I Believe in God, Now What?

Jordone Branch

Copyright © 2015 by Jordone Branch

All rights reserved. No part of this publication may be reproduced, stored in a retrieval system, or transmitted in any form or by any means, electronic, mechanical, recording or otherwise, without the prior, written permission of the publisher.

Published by:
Godly Writes Publishing
P. O. Box 2005
Orangeburg SC 29116-2005

Scripture quotations marked AMP taken from the Amplified® Bible, Copyright © 1954, 1958, 1962, 1964, 1965, 1987 by The Lockman Foundation
Used by permission. www.lockman.org

Unless otherwise noted, scripture quotations are taken from the King James Version of the Bible.
Public Domain.

I BELIEVE IN GOD, NOW WHAT?
ISBN 10: 0970409370
ISBN 13: 978-0-9704093-7-9

COVER DESIGN BY GREG JACKSON, THINKPEN DESIGN

FOR WORLDWIDE DISTRIBUTION, PRINTED IN THE U.S.A.

Dedication

This book is dedicated to Jesus Christ because without Him my life would not be what it is today.

Thank you to my parents: Gregory Branch and Belinda Davis-Branch. You all ensured that I grew up in a church. It's because of those moments that I knew to turn to God during life's toughest circumstances. I love you both.

I'd like to give a special thank you to my future husband, Eddie Massey, III. You've been by my side every step of the way with this book. Thank you for the many hours you spent editing, proofreading, and reminding me of who I am in Christ. I couldn't have done this without you. I love you.

Thank you to my Pastor, Shane Wall, for your dedication to God's work. This book was made possible because of your obedience to God's voice. Thank you also to your wife, Jasmyne Wall, for her ability to love and support you. I love you both.

My acknowledgements wouldn't be complete without thanking my Assistant Pastor, Hayward R. Jean, his wife, Starlette Jean, and their family. Hayward, thank you much for your mentorship, humility, and love. I appreciate all the many hours you've spent trying to guide me in the right direction. I love you and your family very much.

Thank you to my church family at The Feast of the Lord, my sisters, my other family members, my mentors, and my friends. I appreciate all of your love, support, and prayers. I love you all!

Last but certainly not least, thank you to my Jordonewrites.com blog readers! You all began this writing journey with me long before anyone else! Your desire to love God inspires me to continue telling my story. Thank you for your support and prayers. I love you all!

Acknowledgements

Eddie Massey, III
Minister
eddiemassey.com

G. Miki Hayden
Editor

Hayward Jean
Speaker/Minister
haywardjean.com

Zachary Mason
Christian Rapper/Minister
freshfoundationblog.org

Jade Butler
Christian Blogger
hisjoymycrown.com

Latanya Clark
Christian Vendor
facebook.com/youniquesdesign

David C. Marshall, Jr.
Technology Architect
www.davidhelp.me

Dr. Shane Wall
Pastor
shanewall.com

Jasmyne Wall
Artist
Jasmynewall.weebly.com

J.I. Cleveland
Voice Over Artist
facebook.com/jivoice

Table of Contents

Foreword: Getting What We Want from God	ix
Introduction: Wild Goose Chase: Pursuing God Above Everything	xvii
Chapter 1: Believing Isn't Enough	23
Chapter 2: How Could He Be So Heartless?: Forgiving Others	27
Chapter 3: Can You Hear Me Now? Knowing God's Voice for Ourselves	33
Chapter 4: Sowing Great to Be Great	41
Chapter 5: Playing Church: Going Beyond the Four Walls	47
Chapter 6: Independent Woman: You're More Than Your Career	53
Chapter 7: Ugh, I Want Some Sex! Overcoming Temptation	59

Foreword: Getting What We Want from God

One...two...three...four. I counted the ibuprofen pills on my bathroom countertop. Five...six...seven...eight. I kept counting, hoping by the time I reached a certain number, I would change my mind about the drastic decision I was about to make. Countless days of bullying had taken its toll on me. I was only a teenager, but I should have been wise enough to know that no situation is worth my life. I didn't let wisdom have its way that day. I had reached my lowest point of stupidity: I was ready to give up on God.

Nine...ten...eleven. My counting began to frustrate me. I was ready to get it all over with-to be done with it all. So, I downed them all. In my eyes, I was getting even with God. I had *been* praying to Him. I had *been* trying to have faith. But, He wasn't answering my prayers. How was I supposed to have faith in a God that didn't give me what I want? How was I supposed to live for a God that made me suffer? I didn't know that God uses trials to inspire others. I was ignorant to the idea of dying to myself. I thought my belief in God was only about *me*.

Surely, these thirty-one pills would be the cure to all my problems. Surely, giving up on God would be the answer to my difficulties. Indeed, the point of living for God *must* be to receive what *I* wanted from Him. If what I wanted wasn't what was best for me, what was? I didn't know the purpose of living for God: to relinquish my desires for the sake of someone greater than myself. That *someone* was Him. He was greater than me. His way was greater than mine. But, I was ignorant to that reality. Humility was not my best friend. Pride was not my enemy. I was convinced my own way must be better than His. I was wrong. My arrogance almost led me down a path of death. *Almost.*

I was eager to end my life simply because I couldn't get the blessings I wanted from God when I thought I was ready to have them. I was ignorant to Who God is and the way to get Him to answer my prayers. I failed to realize that a relationship with God is not based off what He gives me. God is not my bank and I am not His customer. He does not sit around waiting to serve me. It is I who must serve Him with my prayers, not the other way around.

In the rare moments I did go to Him, there were no conversations, no questions about His will, and no patience to hear His voice, only immediate requests that I *expected* to be answered. I didn't know that the purpose of prayer is to find out what God wants, not for me to recite a list of my desires. Yes, Jesus did say that we should ask, but He also requested that we abide in His will. Abiding in His will isn't limited to our physical lives but includes our prayer lives too.

I didn't understand prayer according to God's perspective. So, whenever my prayers went unanswered, I became frustrated, irritated, and rebellious against God. I brought death into my life through my own disobedient mindset. I was dying inside long before my suicide attempt. There were words in my prayers, but no faith. I was distant from God but didn't realize how distant I really was. I thought going to church was enough to get what I wanted from Him. Even worse, I felt *entitled* to my desires. I

Foreword

was far from humility. I believed in God, but I looked nothing like His Son.

My faith in God was only an extent of my limited relationship with Him. I believed in God, but I didn't *know* Him. So, when life's toughest moments came along, I had nothing to sustain myself. I couldn't stand on His Word because I wasn't living in it. Instead of looking inward, I blamed God. I felt like I wasn't being taken care of by Him because He wasn't handling my life how I wanted Him to. But, the problem wasn't Him, it was me. I didn't know His will for my life or His voice, so I only relied on my own limited understanding of Him to get me through the day. I thought His desires were supposed to match up with mine. What I failed to realize is that God will only give me blessings according to *His will*, not my own. God sees what I can't, and while He knows the future, I don't. He will only give me what's in the best interest of my life and well-being. Oftentimes, what I *want* from God and what I actually *need* from Him are two different things.

Today, I can recognize the blessing in those years of isolation. I am more humble, more loving, and better able to relate to others because of what I went through. That experience taught me to put all my trust in God, instead of what I want from Him. I also learned to love God wherever I am in life, instead of waiting to love Him once He's given me what I want. When I learned to do this, it became easier to see that God's love is *always* around me, despite my situation. We don't have to wait for God's love to show up through our next blessing. His love already exists in our present circumstances. In what we see as lack, God sees as love.

Just because we feel inconvenienced or uncomfortable because of a blessing we don't receive, that doesn't mean we aren't being taken care of by God. If we are His children *and in*

His will, He has already promised to take care of us. Not taking care of us would be going against His Word. But, as Psalms 138:2 tells us, God puts His Word above His name. So, if He says He's going to do something, then He will. However, *He's only responsible for what He says, not what we assume He will give us*.

My attempted suicide taught me how important it is to *only* rely on what God has spoken, and not what I assume He wants for me. I was fortunate to have survived my own stupid decision, but there are others who haven't been as fortunate. People often kill themselves, go crazy, or damage their lives because they relied on their own fabricated thoughts of what they assumed God would give them. They walked around saying, "I believe God is going to give me so and so by next year," but never actually heard God's Word on that circumstance. They wanted something for their lives and used God's name as an excuse to support their fabrication. When the blessing never arrived, they became distraught, disappointed, and lost. But, God never spoke that blessing, it was *only* a desire of *their own*.

Instead of assuming God wants what you want, *wait* to actually hear from Him. Don't say something is "God's will" or that you're "believing in God for something," if you haven't even asked God for His opinion on the matter. Unfortunately, the idea of assuming something is God, without actually asking Him, has become normal. I know because I was a part of that normality. I wasn't living for God, but I used His name to support my ideas, wishes, and endeavors. I had no idea what His will was for my life, but as soon as something came along that I wanted, it all of a sudden became "God's will." Be careful about stating what *you think* God wants for your life. If God hasn't *said* it, don't do it. I know people that have gotten married and moved across

Foreword

the country while stating it was "God's will," when they didn't even know God, have a relationship with Him, or take the time to learn His voice. There is a simple way to avoid this path: only rely and act on what God wants for your life.

Before jumping into a prayer time full of requests, I always ask God, *Daddy, what is your will for this situation? Is it the time for me to receive what I'm asking for? Are these desires I'm feeling yours as well, or are they simply my own?*

I have found that the key to receiving the blessings of God is to pray for *His* will, not my own. Go to God with a purpose of finding out what He wants, not to tell Him what you want. If you ask *and abide* according to His will, you'll always receive what He already has for you. Also, never put God on a time limit in prayer. *Never* tell God you need Him to do something by a certain time period. When your request isn't answered, you'll lose hope because your faith was in the time, not Him. Let God handle the matter His way, not yours.

God wants to bless us. But, He wants to do so when He knows we're prepared to manage and maintain His gifts. I think about the many people who win the lottery for millions of dollars, only to blow it away in less than a year. They got what they wanted, but they weren't prepared to maintain it. Receiving blessings God's way requires patience, but for me, I now find that the wait is always worthwhile. God uses seasons of patience to prune, mold, and shape us into people who are ready to handle all that He has for us. That way, when we get what He wants us to have, *no* man or circumstance will be able to take it away.

In addition to only praying God's will, there is something else we must remember as we talk to God: only pray from a pure, selfless, heart. Ask yourself, *"Why do I want what I want from God?"* In my past, I have oftentimes found myself working hard to achieve a goal that I claimed was for my family and God, but it was really for me. Today, God has blessed me with a different mindset. I often pray that God will allow this book to reach the masses, but it's because I know it has the ability to win souls for His kingdom. I used to pray for finances for worldly success. Now, instead of praying for money, my focus is on how God can use money through me. I ask Him to bless me with wisdom and understanding, so that I can have the knowledge to keep His blessings and be an asset to His Kingdom. Doing well in life is nice, but do we want to reach the top for God's benefit, or simply for our own?

Deepening your relationship with God is the key towards praying selflessly. Although there's nothing wrong with making requests to God that align with His will, the overall focus of our prayer time should never be worldly requests, but spiritual desires. If our relationship with God is strong, then we can learn to be motivated to pray in a Godly manner. *We should pray for spiritual needs more than our human wants.*

Your spiritual prayers should have no limit. Never be shy to ask God for the wisdom, understanding, and insight to handle a situation. What if God gives you the money you need to handle a bill but not the wisdom? You'll only find yourself in that same situation again next month! Sure, you can pay the bill, but what's it worth if you don't understand how to budget your money to avoid that predicament again. More importantly, never hesitate to ask God to help those around you. If you see that your co-worker's life is a hot mess, stop gossiping about her. Instead, pray that God will help her to understand her life according to God's perspective. Pray for wisdom in the life of your wife, family, and friends. A prayer of love for your family can do much more than any monetary amount you can give them. The more genuine and

Foreword

profound our spiritual desires become, the more God can trust us to handle the blessings He already has for us. He'll know that the gifts He gives us won't blind our hearts. In prayer, we must understand that no blessing can ever be more important than sharing the love of God with someone else.

I believe someone was praying for me that I could receive the miracle of God's love. While a blessing is something that we may attribute to man, a miracle like salvation is something only God can take credit for. Jesus performed many miracles, but salvation was the greatest of them all. So, as disciples of His kingdom, we should make the object of our prayers not just our personal wish list, but we ought to include prayers of deliverance for others.

If someone had been more focused on her selfish desires than praying for my salvation, maybe I *wouldn't* have thrown up those pills. Maybe I *wouldn't* be alive today. Yet, through God's grace, and the prayers of others, Jesus saved me! It is my sincere prayer that this book inspires your prayer life and relationship with God. Let's pray for the salvation, deliverance, and spiritual growth of others, and let God take care of meeting our needs just the way He has already promised. I look forward to God blessing you through the words He's allowed me to write in this book....

I love you,
Jordone

A prayer for us to share together...

*Dear God,
I pray that you open my heart to the words I'm about to read. Help me to receive all that you have for me. Help me to know your peace for myself. I want to deepen my relationship and prayer life with you. Thank you for dying so that I may live. In Jesus' name, amen.*

Introduction
Wild Goose Chase: Pursuing God Above Everything

For a moment's time after a sexual orgasm, I would feel great. Yet, only minutes later, I was back to being reminded of my insecurities and the havoc that stemmed from trying to cover them up in the false hope of being saved by idols. I use the term idols because that's exactly what I turned men into. I went to them before I went to God. Although I never said it out loud, my actions proved that I believed those men could heal me in a way that God couldn't. I went running to people, instead of to Him.

I once went on a year-long wild goose chase, pursuing this man who really didn't care to be in a relationship with me. At the time, I was living in Morocco as a Peace Corps volunteer. So, because of the different time zones, I would stay up until all hours of the morning, waiting for a promised call that never came.

Although the numerous missed calls were evidence enough that he didn't care for me, I pressed on. I was determined and assured that this guy was "the one." I wrote him a three-page email expressing my love and desire to marry him, but he didn't even acknowledge the words until three weeks later. Clearly, I was doing more giving than receiving in the relationship, yet I kept running after him anyway.

I was at a point where I would allow myself to be taken advantage of in relationships and so-called friendships because I didn't know my own worth. I also didn't understand the fullness of all that God had in store for me. So, I would settle. I would always allow myself to accept people into my life who did more taking than they did giving. Each relationship was part of an endless cycle of disappointment. Although I didn't realize it, the same treatment that others were giving me was *exactly* how I had treated God.

Prior to my relationship with Him, God was doing all the work. He would bless me with jobs and finances, and even protect me from harm's way when I didn't deserve the protection. I would thank Him, then go on and continue living exactly how I wanted to. I wasn't witnessing or sharing the gospel with others. I preferred a life of sex and lustful pleasures.

God was doing all the giving, and I was doing all the taking. I would look around and see that others weren't loving me the way I deserved, not knowing that my external relationships could only mimic my internal relationship with Christ. How could I understand what I truly deserved if I never spent time with the One Who designed my self-worth?

So, with guy after guy and friend after friend, I would accept the least of my value. To make matters worse, I had a mindset that a man was supposed to be my everything. I didn't know that only God can be my

Introduction

everything. This type of thinking led me to bend over backward, making sacrifices for men who really didn't deserve my time.

Finally, I arrived at the point where I became tired of giving the world what God deserved. It was God who deserved the sacrifice of my body, my time, and my life, not these men. So, I began to learn what sacrifice meant. If I was going to have a relationship with God, I was going to have to stop treating Him the way others had treated me. I began to understand that God has emotions and a personality. Just as I had been hurt by those who'd wronged me, God was hurt by my distance and selfishness.

I yearned for the understanding that only God could be my everything. You see, for so long, my mentality that a one-day spouse could be my all had left me with the false assumption that another human on this Earth could complete me. In reality, no one can complete us; only God can fill that space.

God wanted to be my all. He didn't want me to call men my everything, not because He's bossy, but because He knew thinking that way would cause me to have expectations of men only God could live up to. No one could heal my insecurities, loneliness, depression, and suicidal thoughts. Only God can do that. No amount of intimacy with a significant other can heal what's on the inside of us.

Time and time again, we make sacrifices for people who really don't deserve our love. We break our backs for men and women who could care less about us. In the midst of all this, God sends sign after sign, reminding us that our genuine worth is in Him; yet, we ignore His calls. Yes, there is a reward for sacrifice. But, the true rewards of sacrifice will only come to fruition once we start sacrificing for the One we were created for: God.

We put a great deal of effort into relationships that only last a season. In return, we receive less for our efforts than we expected because we put our all into something that couldn't give us what we were looking for. One relationship after the next, we search for satisfaction in all the wrong places. We think the spouse or friendship that we want will complete us. Yet, months after we receive what we *thought* we wanted, we're back to feeling discontent again. The sacrifices we make for worthless relationships take away time that we should be giving to God.

The completion we long for really lies in having a genuine relationship with Him. As with any relationship, getting to know God will take time and sacrifice. However, unlike the unfulfilled promises of this world, God won't make us sacrifice our time, love, and energy just to leave us disappointed. His miracles will always flow in abundance, according to our obedience.

So, how do our relationships with God look? Is God the only One sacrificing in our lives? Do we make family and friends so much of our everything that God has no room to be our all? Let's step out in faith, obey Him, and make the sacrifices necessary to deepen our relationships with Him. God has boundless gifts waiting for us, but we must have the faith that allows us to receive what He wants us to have. Having that faith will take our sacrifice, but since we sacrifice so much for everything else, why shouldn't we give God the same concern?

1
Believing Isn't Enough

I was living a double life. Everyone knew it except for me. God was my friend, but only on Sundays. Other days, I preferred to live a life of secrecy. I enjoyed God, but only when I needed something. And I was blind to my own faults, so I couldn't understand why my life was in such disarray.

"Why me?" I would ask myself. "What am I doing wrong?" Little did I know, I was paving my own path to destruction.

Before I understood that believing wasn't enough, you would see me in the club with a drink in one hand and weed in the other. Sex was my main stress reliever, but even that wasn't enough. All along, I had no idea that what I was doing was "against God." In my own eyes, I wasn't doing anything wrong. After all, I knew other people in my church who were living that way too.

I didn't know that I couldn't listen to music that shouted "F**k bit***es, get money" while on Sunday listening to the sweet melodies of worship music without having an internal conflict. I hardly even cracked open my Bible unless I had an emergency. I thought believing was enough. I didn't know He wanted my life too.

I Believe in God, Now What?

My crazed habits only intensified as the stress in my life became greater, a stress that I soon realized I was only bringing down on myself. In the middle of living this life that many would consider to be "wild," just about the worst happened to me. I was raped. This was an event I didn't want to look at in my mind, that I wanted to deny, but that brought me deep emotional turmoil in me, a turmoil I very nearly couldn't deal with. I certainly couldn't deal with it as I was, undisciplined and immature, and without really accepting the solace and the peace that God can bring.

Amid the aftermath of being raped, I blamed myself for what had happened. I was dealing with the pain the only way I knew how, through drinking alcohol and smoking weed. Even when I would try to stop one or the other, or both, I couldn't. I had become addicted to the exhilaration that came with each of these substances. Instead of taking my pains to God, I was releasing them in a joint. Only, it wasn't release, it was a vicious cycle of getting high and coming down and having to get high again—an addiction.

One particular night, after I got back to my apartment from the club, I came to my room and prayed on my knees, as I did almost every night before going to sleep.

Watching me, my friend asked, "How can you go from grinding at the club to praying on your knees?"

I said something like, "God knows my heart. Going to the club doesn't mean I don't love Him." I didn't realize it at the time, but that conversation planted a seed in my heart.

From that day on, God began to work on me. He led me to see that the way I was living didn't express to God that I loved Him. I used to think that loving God and even love itself was some type of euphoric feeling. God began to show me that love is an

Believing Isn't Enough

action, not a feeling. It's a verb. Love is demonstrated through what I do, not what I say or how I feel. So, when I say I love God, or anyone for that matter, my love is proven through my actions, not words alone. Clearly, my actions didn't demonstrate that I loved God.

Although my response to my friend was brief, her words really got me pondering about how I might appear to others. Strangely enough, my friend was raped around the same time I was.

In an attempt to encourage her, I would tell her that, "God is going to get you through this," not knowing that she was looking at my life as a statement of my faith and no doubt didn't see much faith in it.

Suddenly, I realized that believing wasn't really enough, nor was helping others enough. Christ didn't die for me to be a charitable citizen. He died for me so that I would have a visible example of what it means to live for God. Through His death, He wanted me to understand that knowing Him is not just about believing, it's about dying to the self.

I had to change my understanding of what living for God means. I thought about what salvation really looks like. If a lifeguard sees me drowning and saves me from death, then I've been pulled out of the water that was taking me down. When I'm saved from worldly activities, I'm no longer drowning in them. The mess of this world— the worrying, the doubt, the drugs, the alcohol, the fornication, and the lies—can no longer consume me. The lifeguard, or Jesus, has given me a second chance at life. That new beginning doesn't include the mess that once tried to bring me down.

Once I was out of my mess, I had to learn to continue to die to myself. Every day brought a new opportunity for God to remove something else out of my heart that separated me from Him. The more I died to myself, the greater my relationship with Him could flourish. The greater our relationship, the better I was able to fully accomplish His will for my life. I had no need to ask whether His way was best because that question was clearly answered through what my past looked like before Him. When I relied on my own desires and intuition, I was drowning.

When I wasn't dying to myself, I allowed little opportunity for God to keep me from the mess He wanted me to avoid. Turmoil followed my disobedience. I was ambitious, did great in school, and had an incredible work experience with notable companies. Yet, I had no peace.

When trouble would come I would say, "It's okay God. I trust you're going to handle this," not knowing that I got myself in that situation because I wasn't living for God in the first place. I treated God like a spare tire. I only used Him for emergencies.

I never realized that I should ask God *before* proceeding with a decision and not just consult Him after the decision had already landed me in a disaster. I wasn't even aware of the concept of going to God outside of making requests. I thought believing in Him was enough. *Now, I understand that something follows after believing and that something is a relationship.*

I found an answer to my problems. I found a release to my stress. I found a healing to my pain. However, I didn't truly find any of these until I learned to give God my all. He doesn't just want our lives so that He can be authoritative. He wants them because He knows that no offering that the world can make contains the peace that only He is able to provide. He wants us to experience relief from what we may be going through, but He can't truly help us until we allow Him to have our *all*. Then and only then will we understand that believing just isn't enough.

2
How Could He Be So Heartless?: Forgiving Others

I was lost and depressed for one main reason: I hadn't forgiven. My wounds were the reason that it didn't take long for the joy of a Sunday morning sermon to leave my heart. By Sunday evening, I was already stressed again and by Monday morning I was smoking another joint to pacify the pain. It was an endless cycle. I would ignore the pain, thinking a sermon could clean it up. I didn't understand that as much as God wanted to heal my hurt, I had a part to play too. He couldn't truly heal me unless I forgave first.

I knew the Lord was opening my heart in a good way the moment I heard myself pray for peace and salvation in the life of the man who raped me. If we can learn to put our pride aside, it's easy to realize that the people who intentionally hurt us need our prayers more than our judgment.

I didn't know just how much pain my rapist kept buried inside of him until about five months after finding out that my case would not proceed to trial. I received a call that I will never forget. It was from my rapist's wife. By this point, I had already found out that he was married at the time of my attack, but I had never expected to hear a phone call from his spouse.

I Believe in God, Now What?

My body tensed as I realized who was on the other end of the call, and my head spun when she mentioned his name. I couldn't understand my emotions and my reaction surprised me. What was all this praying and trusting in God for if all these months had gone by and I could still shake with fear at just the sound of his name? As I asked myself this question, my pastor's statements about forgiveness echoed through my head. "Forgiveness must happen immediately, but healing will take time," he told me one day. They both require extreme amounts of patience. The more time you spend with God, the more patience you acquire, and the easier it becomes for healing to develop.

When I humbled myself by taking my emotions out of the situation, I was able to get my mind together and stay on the phone.

"How do you know my husband?" she asked me.

"Well, to be honest with you, I went on a date with your husband not knowing he was married. During our date, he raped me," I replied in a soft tone.

At first, there was a stark silence on her end. I felt a shock in her voice as she replied, "Oh my gosh. That was you?"

Apparently, she had noticed a piece of mail from the police department notifying him of my intent to press charges. She also overheard him talking with the police who were working on my case. After her discoveries, she was prompted to investigate into the life of her husband. She discovered that he had cheated with 30 other women. His actions had left her with herpes which, by the grace of God, I never received.

She demanded that he give her a list of his phone call and text message history so she could gather evidence for their divorce trial. She went down the list, one by one, calling each woman. I don't know which number I was on the list. I hoped and prayed

How Could He Be So Heartless?: Forgiving Others

that I was the only one who had to endure the physical pain that I experienced.

"What happened with your case? Were you able to take him to court?" she asked me.

"I tried my best, but the state told me that there wasn't enough evidence in my case for me to press charges," I responded.

"Jordone, what's your email? I'm going to send the list of women I told you about so that you can call them to see if you were the only one he did this to. If the other girls are willing to come forward, that could go a long way towards reopening the case," she said.

I looked up at the wall and took a deep breath. To be honest, for a split second, I took the idea into consideration. At that very moment, God reminded me that I prayed to Him to heal my hurt. I recalled the sense of peace I felt after realizing that no jail sentence could ever solve this situation in the way that forgiveness could. I didn't want to pursue punishing my attacker anymore. I wanted to forgive him and move on by praying for his salvation. Love had interceded in a place that evil first resided and I wanted to leave it at that. I had learned to allow my prayers to conquer my pain, not a tiresome and stressful path of revenge.

I'm not knocking those who decide to pursue pressing charges against those who have wronged them. Everyone's situation can be dealt with differently according to God's will. But for me, I was content knowing that the peace, understanding, and insight I had attained during that ordeal allowed me to forgive not only my attacker, but the many other people whose wrongs against me I had buried on my heart. So, I politely declined her offer.

As I spoke, I could hear their newborn baby crying in the background. It was almost as if the baby's wails were coming from her mother's heart. I could sense the depth of hurt that she was experiencing. Her pain seemed so much greater than mine. I wasn't raising his child, I didn't have herpes, and I was never deceived by him in the way that she was.

The tone of her voice let me know that her hurt had turned into bitterness. She was angry with him. She craved revenge. At one point, so did I. Since I had learned through prayer that these feelings do nothing to solve the situation, I asked her if she wanted to pray together. She accepted. We prayed for her hurt, for my hurt, for the hurt her children would one day experience as a result of this divorce and, most importantly, for the person who had more hurt than any of us—him.

We have to let God be the One to rip out all the pain that's on the inside of us, but He can't heal us unless we let go of our wounds. Sometimes, the most hurtful wounds are those we cause ourselves by not letting go of the path that God is begging us to leave. How can God help us to forgive unless He has our lives, and how can He have our lives if we are still living our own way? In order for God to replace the voids in our lives with His love, we must yield our *entire* minds and hearts to Him. I couldn't have fully forgiven my attacker if my mind was still focused on sinning. I would have been on the same path of heartache and disappointment, not making myself fully available to receive from the Lord. Likewise, simply going to church would have never healed my pain either. The forgiveness God wanted me to have came with an obedience to live His will. The ability to let go lies within seeking a relationship with God.

As we struggle with the aftermath of the hurt we feel from a situation, we surely want to remember the suffering Christ endured on the cross for all of us. He experienced the ultimate pain, even though He knew we would take His efforts for granted. He loves us *beyond* our flaws. Now, as we walk in Christ, we must

How Could He Be So Heartless?: Forgiving Others

follow His example by loving those who have hurt us. Loving those who love us back is easy. The ultimate form of love is to love those who have hurt us. We want to have patience with them, forgive them, pray for them, and give ourselves time to heal.

Love endures long and is patient and kind...
1 Corinthians 13:4 (AMP)

3
Can You Hear Me Now? Knowing God's Voice for Ourselves

I can recall the first time I stepped out in faith to obey God's commands. As I stood in a gas station, I could hear His voice telling me to approach and pray for a woman who was standing near me. I was ready to walk away in fear. After all, I had never even met this woman and I knew nothing about her. As I inched closer towards her, the fear inside of me began to lead my footsteps in the opposite direction. Then, out of nowhere, a wave of courage came over me. I turned around and began to walk her way again. Instead of following my own desires, I decided to walk out in faith.

After casually introducing myself, I simply said, "I feel as though the Holy Spirit is telling me to pray with you. Do you want to pray together?"

In a pleasant and grateful tone, she responded, "You heard right, I really need it."

As we stood praying together, the Lord began to tell me details about this woman's life that I could have never known on my own.

"Were you recently raped?" I asked her in a soft tone.

I Believe in God, Now What?

I guess she was speechless because, with a shocked face, she looked at me and responded *yes* by slowly nodding her head.

Having previously been raped myself, I knew that God would use my testimony to inspire her. I told her she could conquer what she was going through. I let her know I was a living testimony that such a dreadful experience could bring her closer to God. A stream of tears began to roll down her face. Then, God also began using me to encourage her to not commit suicide. I shared with her that my rape had also brought me to suicidal thoughts, and that killing herself would only eliminate the chance of seeing her situation improve.

If I hadn't obeyed God's command to pray with that woman, she might not be alive today. Obedience to God is a requirement for every command because we never know His entire reasoning for telling us to do something. My small step of obedience that day ended up saving someone's life, but I never would have known that it was God speaking to me if I hadn't been spending so much time with His Word.

God's voice is in His Word- the Bible. When we don't know or believe His Word, we become deaf to His voice. When it comes to knowing God's voice, it's not enough to simply memorize scriptures. Plenty of people can repeat scriptures left and right, yet they have no faith. God's voice is in the knowledge *and* belief of Who He is.

God's voice is also in a relationship with Him. How can we know someone's voice if we've never spent time with them? If a good friend calls me on the phone, I know who's on the other line as soon as they say "hello." I don't need caller ID to recognize who they are because we've spent so many quality moments together. I would willingly carry on a conversation and take vital life advice from that caller without them ever

Can You Hear Me Now? Knowing God's Voice for Ourselves

identifying themselves, simply because I know their voice and believe who they are. Likewise, knowing God's voice comes with a relationship with Him. We can recognize His voice, His advice, and His commands once we've spent more time with Him. His Word is the core towards knowing Who He is and building that special bond with Him.

Oftentimes, we ask God to answer questions about our lives. In many instances, He answers, but His words fall on deaf ears that don't know His voice. He speaks, but we don't recognize His voice because we don't know Him. If it were a friend speaking, we would have clearly heard the advice and adhered. Sadly, we know our friends better than we know God, which is why we run to them for advice when we *think* He doesn't hear us. But, He *does* hear us. It's *us* that don't hear Him. If we want to know what God is saying about our situations, all we have to do is spend time with the Bible and act obediently to what it says. The more we listen to Him in the small areas of our lives, the easier it becomes to understand His directions for larger matters.

> *My sheep hear my voice, and I know them, and they follow me.*
> John 10:27

Once I knew what I needed to do to hear God's voice, I decided to change to a church that focused on building a relationship with Him. At the time, the idea of God having a voice was still new to me. Yet all the church members around me were already familiar with hearing Him in that way.

Everyone in my new church would come in with testimonies, saying, "God told me this and God told me that," and I would sit there in awe.

I Believe in God, Now What?

I would think, *What do they mean God told them something?* It was clear to me that my spiritual life was missing an ingredient that they already had—a deep relationship with God. Desperate for God to heal my wounds, I had spent months after being raped trying to get to know Him better, but I had yet to make an attempt to hear His voice. It was *only* me who was doing all the talking during our prayer time together. Imagine being in a marriage where your spouse refuses to listen and always dominates the conversation. That would be a very difficult, one-sided relationship. Yet, that's how I treated God. *You can't have a relationship with someone if you're the only one who does the talking.* Relationships can only develop once the communication from *both* parties grows.

My new pastor was encouraging me to pray in a way I had never even thought of. "Jordone," he would kindly tell me. "Your prayers should be a conversation, not a speech."

So, I began to try to have that conversation. Instead of just going to God with a list of requests, I would say, "God, how do you want me to pray about this situation?" Then, I would wait for an answer. Yet, I oftentimes found myself feeling frustrated. I seemed to be making a tremendous effort to hear from God, but He wasn't saying anything back. I would spend day and night trying to hear His voice. I soon found out that I was trying too hard.

> *Do not fret or have any anxiety about anything, but in every circumstance and in everything, by prayer and petition (definite requests), with thanksgiving, continue to make your wants known to God.*
> Philippians 4:6 (AMP)

Can You Hear Me Now? Knowing God's Voice for Ourselves

God doesn't want us to be anxious to hear from Him. He's my Father, not a celebrity. So, my conversations with Him should be personal, not filled with anxiety. He doesn't want us to be worried about whether or not we'll hear His voice. So, we should never go into prayer with an attitude of, "God, if you don't tell me how I'm going to pay this, I don't know what I'm going to do!" That's not faith. That's operating out of frustration and fear. He just wants to communicate with us as though we're His children. He would rather not speak than for us to be anxious. After all, He's not just God—He's our Dad too. He wants you to hear from Him, but He also wants to be sure you trust Him as a Father too.

So, I calmed down and prayed without the expectation of fireworks. Instead, I just had the expectation of a voice—a calming, loving voice. When we can simply talk to God with a heart of "Hi, Dad. I know you love me," we can have an understanding of His true and loving character. He doesn't want to only hear requests from us, He wants to hear that He is loved. We are made in His image. So, if we don't want one-sided, request-filled, unloving relationships, then neither does He. If we love to hear that we are loved, then so does He. Our time with God should never end. Our relationship with Him is a marriage. Just like a spouse, He wants to be included in *every* part of our lives.

Pray without ceasing.
1 Thessalonians 5:17

To include God in every part of our day, we should be talking to Him throughout the day, not just during a set prayer time. When I first started nurturing my relationship with God, I used to spend time with Him every morning and evening. But, throughout the day we did no talking. So, my time with Him was more like a schedule than a relationship. Of course, if you had a preference, you would never want to hear from your spouse only during scheduled times. Our times with Him should feel like a marriage, not a meeting.

God wants to hear from us consistently. Talk to Him about what you're doing. I don't mean small talk, I mean use your time with Him to change the world. Instead of thinking about how your boss is getting on your nerves, pray for her. Instead of thinking about your to-do list, pray about it. Instead of thinking about your husband and children, pray for them. Your prayers are much more powerful than your thoughts. So, turn your thoughts into prayers. *Half the time that we are thinking, we should actually be praying.*

Spending consistent time with God during each day is better than merely running to Him when trouble occurs. When we run to God in haste only because of an emergency, we'll have difficulty hearing from Him because we don't have a close relationship with Him. If we build a relationship with Him, we can experience the constant comfort of knowing what God wants in every situation. We'll know exactly what He's saying and which path to take.

Once God speaks to us, we must be sure to obey. As we make a habit of obeying the directions that God gives us, we're able to understand and hear from Him more clearly. If God commands us to do something, but we only listen to our own desires, properly identifying when God is speaking to us, versus when we're listening to our human selves, can be difficult.

Sometimes God may answer us, but other times He will expect us to wait. The more we go to Him, the more consistently we can expect His replies to come. Remember, we should be more concerned about seeking Him than His answers to our requests. Waiting for His replies not only teaches us patience, but also teaches us how to go to Him without fail about everything in faith. So, we don't need to fret if He doesn't reply immediately. Instead, we can just enjoy the ability to spend time in His presence.

Above all else, we ought to remember that each conversation with God should begin in praise, repentance, and openness. When we're open, we aren't thinking about our day or to-do lists, we're focused and ready to receive what God has for us.

Still, if at the start, we make the mistake of confusing God's voice with our own, we can't let that discourage us from continuing to pursue a relationship with Him. We need to keep speaking and listening to Him. Just as with any other friend, the more you speak with Him, the better you'll know Him. You don't normally tell all your secrets to someone once you first meet them. Instead, you begin to talk to them more as the relationship grows. God is the same way. Allow time for your relationship with Him to develop. Don't be in a rush to grow. Enjoy each phase of time with Him and be patient. Go to God in prayer right now. Seek His face and enjoy His presence. Ask Him, "God, what are your concerns? What is your will? How do you want me to pray for myself and others? Show me the way."

4
Sowing Great to Be Great

> *[Remember] this: he who sows sparingly and grudgingly will also reap sparingly and grudgingly, and he who sows generously [that blessings may come to someone] will also reap generously and with blessings.*
>
> 2 Corinthians 9:6 (AMP)

It was November 2013. Approximately one year after I was raped. One year after beginning my relationship with God. One year after giving up my many addictions. Yet, I was still in bondage. Yes, I was free from the captivity of looking for release in my next joint or glass of vodka. But, my mind was still in slavery. I was full of pride and lacking faith. Yes, I had been delivered from the slavery of sin, but my mind was still at the plantation. My mentality and heart had yet to catch up with where my body was going.

It was as if God had dug me out from the graveyard, but I was still stuck on my dead ways. I may have given up the many pleasures that separated me from Him, but my ways of thinking were no better off than my past. For years, I had found security in my paycheck, not Him. My pride was always in the worldly essentials which I found strength in. My job, my resume, and my accomplishments all made me feel like I was somebody. In the midst of finding God, I was ready for Him to strip me of my selfish actions, but not my selfish mindset. Letting go of the addictions that were clearly beginning to eat my life away was easy. Letting go of a mind I had held onto for so long was much harder.

I *enjoyed* thinking my accomplishments made me somebody. I *liked* the comfort of knowing I could always find security in a paycheck. I could grow full off the idea of having my own finances and lucrative bank account. In my own mind, there was no need to change my mentality. My arrogance told me that since I had given up so much for God, I was in perfect standing with Him. I was oblivious to the errors in my own heart. Somehow, I thought that a relationship with God stops at the point of salvation. God had saved me from drugs and sexual addictions, and I thought that was enough. I neglected to realize that there's much more to do after you pick up your cross. Afterwards, you must carry it too.

In order to carry my cross, God had to transform my mind. It wasn't enough to love Him with my actions if He didn't have my mind too. My heart was still fixated on the idea that my worth came from dollar signs. After all He had delivered me from, I *still* had more faith in my paycheck than I did Him. Pride was the error of my ways. He had to rid me of the god that was taking over my life: money. So, he began to take me on a journey of faith.

I spent a year and a half without a steady paycheck. Actually, even as I write these very words, I am still unsure of how God will fund this book. I just know He'll make a way. Many months, I received checks as low as fifteen and thirty dollars for a month's worth of work. I went from making twenty dollars an hour to receiving less than twenty in one month. I lived off of tight budgets and borrowing. Despite my scarcity in funds, God was still commanding me to sow large seeds in faith. He was teaching me that my source is Him, not my income. My relationship with God was no longer limited to a life without sin. There was more He needed me to learn about Him. He had tackled the issues of my sin, now it was time to declare my mind free too.

One after the other, I felt led to sow large seeds. When you've only made twenty dollars for a month's worth of work, sowing ten feels like a heavy weight to give. But, that was my problem: my focus was on the little I had, not the greater He was trying to bring forth. If my faith was in God, giving to Him would never feel like a burden. Tithing isn't a frustration, it's an investment. It wasn't enough that I had learned to stop sinning if my heart was still in the wrong place; the freeing of my actions is just as important as the liberation of my mind. How could I truly declare myself free if my faith was still in wealth? What good was my relationship with God if He could bring me out of slavery, but I couldn't even trust Him to pay a bill?

I was learning that the fruition of salvation extends well beyond avoiding drinking and smoking. God wanted me to have His peace daily, but I had a part to play too. I had to be willing to give up that which was blocking me from total contentment in Him: my mind. God wanted me to experience His love in totality, but He couldn't do that if my mentality kept me from experiencing His greatness. If I was going to know Him as peace, He had to get rid of my mindset that equated money *as* peace. I was learning that there was more to give up even after the battles of temptation ended, but those sacrifices only resulted in great rewards.

I Believe in God, Now What?

Each day presented a new opportunity to trust Him. With only ten dollars in my account, I oftentimes didn't know where my gas or grocery money would come from. But, regardless of the amount I made, I continued to obey His command to sow. Every time I gave in obedience, I always reaped more in return. One day, a friend randomly told me she wanted to buy my groceries. Another day, a church member, who had no idea about the state of my finances, decided to bless me with hundreds of dollars of clothes. During my financial difficulties, there wasn't one day that I ran out of gas or went to bed starving. God *always* made a way to provide. More importantly, He wasn't just providing my needs, He was also providing me with peace. He was removing my god so that He could become my God. In Him was the peace I always lacked. But, in order to receive His peace, I had to obey His commands.

I was finally beginning to understand that God would always take care of my necessities. It's not my necessities I need to obey, but Him. My cares didn't need to be in my gas tank or my wallet, but in Him. My giving opened up doors for Him to bless me with even greater than I could have done for myself. It was never about the amount to God. It was always about my obedience. *In my obedience was my faith.* Through my faith, He could begin to work on my behalf.

That journey of faith without a steady paycheck was exactly what I needed in my life. Prior to that time, my mind was much more focused on my bills than my God. That year taught me to stop placing limits on Him. I had trusted God to deliver me from the evil of this world, but my limited mindset caused me to close doors that He wanted open. I didn't recognize all that He was capable of doing because I was too focused on my surroundings. I had to learn that when I give, I'm not just giving to the

Sowing Great to Be Great

institution of a church, but rather I'm sowing into the spiritual advancement of both myself and those around me. Anytime I refused to step out on faith to obey God with my time, energy, or giving, my disobedience would always affect someone else other than myself.

As we begin to sow with a heart for God, the Lord will reveal to us where to sow, and how the seed should be planted. If we want to reap greater rewards, we must sow greater. If we want a nonprofit, we should sow our time into one. If we want more people to grow in God, we should sow into a ministry that's helping us be greater in God. I'm not saying we shouldn't be wise in our giving with an eye to our own needs, but we should always be obedient as the Holy Spirit leads us.

In order to obey God in our giving, we must be prepared for Him to free our minds. Is your mind like my former self? Has God delivered you from the perils of sin but you *still* don't trust Him to do even greater through your finances? Let's trust the certainty of Him, not the uncertainty of wealth or material items. When we sow, we always reap more than we expected. The Giver is God, not a human. So, when we give to Him, the possibilities of what we might receive in return are infinite. Will you let God have your sins *and* your mind too? If you've fallen in faith, don't beat yourself up. Go to Him in repentance now. Tell Him, "God, I want to love you over money. Help me change my mindset. I trust you, Lord. Please lead the way."

> *Jesus said unto him, Thou shalt love the Lord thy God with all thy heart, and with all thy soul, and with all thy mind. This is the first and great commandment.*
> Matthew 22:37-38

5
Playing Church: Going Beyond the Four Walls

"Just kill yourself and it will all be over," a thought told me.

It was late 2014. I had given my life to God, yet I was still depressed. I was living righteously, yet I had no faith. I was witnessing, yet I didn't believe my own words. My bills were backed up, my payments were late, and there were still no opportunities for employment in my sight. Suicidal thoughts had become my ally. Once I even recall tying a belt around my neck. Other times, I had random thoughts about driving into a tree. I covered my emotions up, but my true friends could see straight through my smiling facade.

Every Sunday sermon filled me with deliverance, peace, and joy, but I was depressed again by Sunday afternoon. Those around me were getting jobs and moving up in life. I felt stuck, almost as if God had forgotten about me. God had taken *everything* from me. Rather, He had taken what I *perceived* as everything. For so long, titles, positions, and money had empowered me. I was a hypocrite: declaring belief in Jesus for others, yet not *acting* upon that belief in my own life. I had told others that God was their everything. But, I clearly didn't believe my own words.

I Believe in God, Now What?

God had stripped me of my assets so that He could become my *only* asset. He was preparing me for greater, but He needed to know that I was ready. He wanted to ensure that my value was in Him, and not the blessings He had for me. I was excited for all He had for me on Sunday morning. But, I was lost again by Monday afternoon. I *knew* the afflictions He had placed before me were in my best interest, but I didn't *believe*. So, I fought Him the whole way.

I had become addicted to the peace of a sermon, but I wasn't living in the words I was taught. I hadn't backslid into the world, but my mind had. I wasn't living church. I was playing church. My actions showed the same worship singing, gospel filled, tongues-praying woman, but I was more reliant on the gifts than the Giver Himself. I *knew* God had plans for my life. Every prophecy I received from God let me know about the high places He was taking me. But, I was frustrated that my blessings were attached to my afflictions. I was irritated that I had to endure suffering, patience, and growth in order to move further. My greatest enemy wasn't the devil, but myself.

Somehow, I thought I was special. I thought knowing God *entitled* me to His blessings. I forgot that everything from God was given to me by grace, not justice. I wasn't always honest with myself about my true sentiments. Oftentimes, I didn't know what my true feelings meant. This intense level of depression was new to me. It was powerful, sporadic, and quickly taking over my life. I was still praying, reading scriptures, and trying to have faith. So, I couldn't understand why I was missing the peace my pastor had promised me every Sunday morning. Yes, I had His peace during church. But, that wasn't enough. Christ didn't die so that my church attendance could be peaceful. He died so that my life could be peaceful.

Playing Church: Going Beyond the Four Walls

After some time, I came to understand the root of my depression: my love for God wasn't personal. My pastor, parents, and friends had all declared that they love God, so I followed their words. But, I had yet to *know* Him for myself. My love for God wasn't based off personal knowledge, but popular opinion. I had been taught to say I trust God, but I didn't understand what that truly meant. I had read countless scriptures that told me to place all my faith in Him. But, I had yet to spend enough time with Him to actually trust that He could handle my life. For so many years, I realized I was only *saying* I trusted God. But, I still didn't *believe* His Word. I had accepted Christ, worshipped in tongues, and fallen out in church. Yet, I still didn't know God for myself. I hadn't spent enough hours before His face on my own.

The cure to my dilemma was simple: I needed to spend more personal time with God. If I continued to live off my pastor's relationship with God, I would never have peace outside the four walls of the church. It was time to start believing God for myself. Having personal time with Him twice a day wasn't enough to know Him as my Savior. It was time to start seeking His face for *hours*. It was time for me to start trusting God for myself. But, I was never going to do that unless I *knew* Him.

So, I thought about what getting to know someone actually looks like. I started thinking about all my past boyfriends I thought I was going to marry. In an effort to know them better, I spent hours on the phone. We each sought multiple ways to know one another, even putting aside our important schedules for the sake of spending more hours together. I began to *trust* those boyfriends because I thought I *knew* who they were. I thought I knew them because I had spent hours with them. Our trust developed as our time with each other developed. Yet, I hadn't given God the same concern. I thought I could trust God *before* knowing Him. I failed to realize that trust only comes with knowledge. Likewise, knowledge only comes with time.

Initially, when I first accepted Christ, I would spend *hours* in prayer and scriptures. Yet, somewhere in the midst of life's trials, busy schedules, and opportunities, my time with God began to dwindle. As our time together decreased, my thoughts about my bills, payments, and job search increased. Gradually, my focus shifted from my God to my problems. Soon enough, my problems had become my god. Yet, I was oblivious to how far I had strayed from Him. I was still praying, but His presence wasn't in my prayers. I was still attending church, but my mind was on myself. God wasn't responsible for my depression or lack of peace. I was. It wasn't Him who had strayed away. It was me.

The promised peace my pastor preached about was and still is mine. But, I wasn't going to receive that peace unless I *knew* God for myself. Knowing Him isn't just about our initial moments together. Knowing Him is about consistency. By stripping me of what I thought was everything, God was allowing me to know Him. He was trying to take the place of the many voids I was unaware of. But, I had to stop fighting Him. In order to have His peace, I had a part to play. I had to let go. Most of all, I had to put the time in with Him.

True trust in God will only occur once we've spent ample time with Him. When I was depressed, my problem wasn't my lack of salvation or church attendance. My problem was I didn't know God enough to trust Him. God had saved me, but our relationship status was still on the stranger level. For the many of us that are saved, yet lacking peace, we have to ask ourselves: where is our time going?

To know God is to trust Him. But, trusting Him requires time with Him. As my pastor once told me, "you will only act

Playing Church: Going Beyond the Four Walls

on what you believe." How can I truly believe and trust God if I haven't gotten to know Him for myself? For so long, I thought I knew God, but I was only relying on the beliefs of others. When trials came in my own life, I realized I didn't know Him as well as I thought. Today, I am a new person. But, it's only because I spent *hours* in God's face. We spend hours on our relationships, jobs, and children because they're important to us. So, why not give God the same concern?

Our lives should say more than, "I believe in God, I go to church, and I'm kind to others." In order to truly feel God's love and peace, our lives must say, "I have a relationship with God. I spend time with Him. I'm obedient to Him. I witness to others and my life is about much more than just church on Sunday."

Christ *is* the way to have peace through *any* situation. But, that peace won't occur unless we trust God for ourselves. If we really believe something, we won't doubt what we've been told. When we know God, there's no lack of faith about what He's doing in our lives. Let's increase our personal time with God so that we can know Him for ourselves. Once we trust God with the whole of our hearts, we can go share the message of Who He is to others. The more we do this, we'll be able to watch as God's everlasting peace surrounds us. We'll experience no doubting and no lack of spiritual discernment. We will have no voids to fill. Our lives will be full of peace, and others will say, "Wow, I want what they have!"

6
Independent Woman: You're More Than Your Career

Before my relationship with God, I always used my personal success to cover up my insecurities. I recall one summer, I got the internship of my dreams at CNN. I was in shackles and a business suit. Yet, nobody knew except for me. I was using so much weed to pacify my pain that smoking became necessary for me to do everyday tasks. Ambitions and goals were just as much of an escape as marijuana. I had a life of bondage where everything looked great on paper, but worse in reality. Everyone except God was marveled by my life. Once a producer even told me, "You've impressed so many people here at CNN. You should be proud."

My family and friends would praise me for my impressive resume, but my personal life was in shambles. Everyone who knew me saw success because they looked at my great professional life, but their sight was only skin deep. Success in the eyes of God is much more.

By the end of college, I had interned with CNN for three consecutive summers. I was using my spare time to network with as many people as I could find. I placed my hope in the titles and positions of other people. I was all over the place, never consulting God before making a move. *My belief was in God, but my faith was in man.* Although I said I trusted the Lord, my actions stated otherwise. I spent a great deal of time trying to build relationships with people, but I never stopped to work on my relationship with God.

I treated people as though they were my source of income and God as if He had the responsibility of adhering to *my* every move. No one knew that my personal life was a wreck. Even in the midst of my havoc, people consistently reminded me what a great future I was going to have. Their comments taught me how different the world's idea of success is from God's version of success. While the world may look at our resumes, God will judge our hearts.

> *Every way of a man is right in his own eyes: but the* Lord *pondereth the hearts.*
> Proverbs 21:2

Sure, I was charitable and looking out for the cares of others, but in God's eyes that's not enough. How could I say that I was doing God's work if my own life didn't reflect faith in His Word? Many of us look at our positive actions and say, "Overall, I mean well. God knows my heart," but the Bible clearly says the heart of man is wicked, which is why we needed Christ to die for us. Having a superb resume and working hard for my family doesn't purify my heart. Working hard for God isn't the key to living righteously. I can work my butt off for God, preach a thousand sermons, be a great wife, and still not enter heaven because of all the unforgiveness and pride in my heart. The cross serves as an intercession for our hearts, not just our actions. It's only when we allow our hearts to *completely* abide in Him that true righteousness in our actions can follow. Completely abiding in Him means placing total trust in Him over our positions in life.

> *The heart is deceitful above all things, and desperately wicked: who can know it?*
> Jeremiah 17:9

When we stand before God, we have to understand that He will judge the details of our lives that we *choose* not to pay attention to. God wants the entirety of our lives, which includes the weaknesses that we overlook as being minor. One of the major weaknesses I had was not trusting God with my professional life. I wanted success, but I wanted to do it the world's way. More specifically, I valued worldly success over Him. Yes, I was a kind person, but my heart was still wicked because my trust was in man, not God. I was only living according to my goals, not my God. Eventually, my goals became my god.

I could only *hope* that the goals I was committing to would work out. I drafted plans and put forth the effort to complete those goals. But, I could still only rely on my own hopes, not God's. I may have prayed about the goal *after* my decision was already made, but I never consulted God *beforehand* to see if my hope was even His will.

All along, I walked around saying, "I know you're going to take care of this for me God. I know you're going to work this one out," but I never stopped to realize that perhaps that idea was my own will, not God's. How can God touch what He isn't even involved in? Oftentimes, we have great ideas, but, as a pastor once told me, every great idea is *not* a Godly idea. On the other hand, every Godly idea will always be a great idea.

I Believe in God, Now What?

I had to change the way I view "God's will," because I always assumed that His purpose would line up with my own desires. I learned to seek God for His understanding of every situation *beforehand*. As His servant, I live for Him, not myself. Committing to a goal that's God's will for my life will always provide me with His favor. When I have God's understanding of how something should be done, I eliminate stress because the hard work has already been performed for me. Once I know that I'm handling an endeavor His way, all that's left to do is to let His work flow through me and watch the blessings come forth.

Committing to goals in an ungodly way will always equal more responsibility and stress on our shoulders. Most people live their lives giving their money, time, and effort toward something they can only hope will work out. Taking a risk for God isn't a gamble. It's an investment. When we have God's approval, we don't just hope, we know.

The worst part of handling success the worldly way is that all the stress we go through amounts to nothing. Sure, God may use our mistakes to work for His kingdom, but ultimately we won't receive the fulfillment He has prepared for us. God's purpose for our lives is attached to our obedience to Him, not our own will.

We have to understand that careers are only a part of our lives' process of spiritual development; they aren't the whole of our lives. Whether you are working or unemployed, you are where you are because someone needs Jesus, not because you need a paycheck. As children of God, we aren't defined by our jobs or retirement status, but by Him. The positions God intends for us can only be received once we truly understand that God is what fulfills us, not a title. We can't look to people and networking groups for our next big break. We have to show God we know that, although He may use others to bless us, the blessings are ultimately from Him. We should look to Him for help first, not people.

Many of us are "successful," yet still feel lost because we aren't listening to God. We arrive home at night not understanding why we worked so hard for everything we *thought* we wanted, yet we still don't feel complete. We handle stress by going to happy hours, wine and dines, and cocktail mixers, but we have no peace. We cast our cares on a bottle of wine, instead of God. The people around us deem it okay because it's socially acceptable, but if we always take our hard day out on a glass of wine, the stress will never go away. The alcohol only suppresses the feelings we should be giving to God.

Through God, we have the ability to stop relying on chance, and start relying on Him—but our works have to be accomplished *His* way. We need to ask God, "Lord, what's your purpose for my life? I want to be complete." If He answers immediately, that's great. If not, patiently wait for His answer. We need to trust Him and not rush out on our own understanding. Doing things God's way is not a gamble, it's a guarantee.

7
Ugh, I Want Some Sex! Overcoming Temptation

To my surprise, the moment I decided that I was done with my old ways, temptation came flooding in. I'd quit smoking weed, but that didn't stop old friends from asking me to smoke. I had let go of the guys I'd had sex with, but their texts seemed to be glued into my phone. Instead of entertaining them, I would ignore them.

Yes, I was still feeling the temptations, but God had taught me that I'm more than just a body. I'm a spirit. The moment I felt an urge, I would quote scriptures and pray for strength. Then, I would *apply* that scripture to my lustful craving. I would shift my mindset from my desire to have sex to my desire to have Jesus. Almost instantly, I would feel my spirit fighting the battle that my body couldn't. God was teaching me that when my body feels weak, it's the Holy Spirit that makes me stronger.

I can recall one particular time where I was extremely turned on. I would get up to distract myself, but the sexual desire was still there. I was tired of living for myself and I was ready to live for God alone. I really didn't want to mess up again. So, I prayed. I said, "God, I know this temptation isn't stronger than you. I know you have power over this feeling. Please give me strength and help me fight this battle. I can't do this without you."

I Believe in God, Now What?

The moment I ended my prayer, all the sexual desires I was feeling faded away. I was amazed because I never witnessed a prayer being answered so quickly. God Himself removed the temptation I was feeling, but He couldn't have done that unless I asked Him for help. Oftentimes, we are too quick to try to fight every battle on our own. We get so comfortable with God that we forget it's *not* us that's strong, it's *Him* Who's strong within us. God has promised to never leave us or forsake us. So, if we have the God of the universe within us, why are we trying to do things on our own? In many instances, God is eager to help us. He's just waiting for us to ask.

> *There hath no temptation taken you but such as is common to man: but God is faithful, who will not suffer you to be tempted above that ye are able; but will with the temptation also make a way to escape, that ye may be able to bear it.*
>
> 1 Corinthians 10:13

As we see from the scripture above, God will do more than just help you through temptation. With every temptation, He will always provide a way out. Oftentimes, that way out is more straightforward than we realize. If you want to know how to leave that man's house, simply use the front door. If you want to know how to stop using alcohol to relieve your stress, start with pouring out all your wine bottles. If you think a certain TV show is keeping your heart from God, turn off the cable. If you don't know how to stop paying for sex, ask God to lead you to an accountability partner that can help you lead the way.

Ugh, I Want Some Sex! Overcoming Temptation

When you're saved, that temptation is much smaller than the strength of Jesus in you. But, the devil will mess with your emotions, feelings, and desires in a way that magnifies the situation. Escaping temptation may be hard, but it's not complicated. You just have to believe that He can fight the battle. Trust Him. Then, take the way out He offers you. When we decide to live for God, *we show God that our faith in Him is greater than the temptation itself.*

Once we are ready to trust God with our temptations, we have to eliminate any culprits that act as an ally to that temptation. A culprit can be anyone, including yourself. Of course, you can't remove yourself from your own life. But, you can ask God daily to remove anything out of your heart that hinders your growth in Him. For me, my culprit is pride. Pride is the mean by which Satan tries to convince me that I can make my own decisions and go my own way, without God. God is currently working on me daily to teach me that I can't rule my life better than He can.

When our own hearts aren't an idol of temptation to us, those closest to us are. We must remove ourselves from environments and people who aren't positive influences, even family and other church members. If they aren't encouraging what God has called you to do, leave them alone. Period. I'm not saying to be rude, nasty, or avoid helping someone that God has called you to assist. Be led of the Holy Spirit. If you feel the need to show someone God's love through your time and actions, just be sure to bring them into your environment, not theirs. Remember, the stronger you become in God, the better you're able to help that family member in need of salvation. But, how can you help them if you're constantly putting yourself in situations that make the *both* of you weaker? Bringing someone to God should never require you to sacrifice your relationship with Christ.

I Believe in God, Now What?

Once you've learned how to overcome temptation, you're ready for a new challenge: being misunderstood. As old friends and family members recognize your Godly choices, you may begin to feel alienated. Suddenly, people who used to talk to you for hours now seem to have nothing in common with you. Old friends who used to party with you are now labeling you as 'holier than thou.' Girlfriends who loved to gossip with you now look at you strange because their gossip has become your prayers.

Everywhere you turn, no one understands you but God. In a moment's glimpse, Satan can use this alienation to turn you away from God and back to your old ways. Don't fall into his trap! Conforming to the world is not the proper response to handle rejection. Keep your standards and remain strong. Remember, this walk is not about you, it's about the One Who has sent you. If someone mocks or rejects you, they aren't doing so to you, they're doing so to God.

> *"Let no one say when he is tempted, I am tempted from God; for God is incapable of being tempted by [what is] evil and He Himself tempts no one"*
>
> James 1:13. (AMP)

Always remember: temptation is *not* punishment from God. I used to ask God, *"Daddy, if you love me so much, why do you tempt me? How could you let me go through this? What did I do wrong?"* I didn't understand that it's never God who tempts me. I also didn't know that living for God doesn't make me immune to new temptations. I was learning that no battle fought for God is futile. When temptation is won, the victory can always prepare you for the next phase of life. God may allow a temptation because He knows overcoming its power will make us stronger, but He'll never be the one to tempt us. God already knows that you can pass any test you're given through Him, so He has no need to tempt you. Satan, on the other hand, is not all knowing, so he's tempting you with the hope that you'll fail.

Passing any test of temptation is all about God giving you a testimony. You can't only live off of your preacher's victories in God. You must have *your own* testimony. It's only through picking up your own cross that you can grow closer to God and have a testimony to share with others. I love my pastor's sermons, but I would have never gotten closer to God if I didn't have my own testimonies about what God has allowed me to conquer.

God wants to use you to minister to souls, but He wants you to be able to give your own account for what He's done in your life. He needs you to have *your own* experience with Him. God would never put you through anything without purpose. He knows that giving you a testimony is one of the surest ways to build your faith and the faith of others. So, stop looking at temptation and trials as a time to grumble. Instead, begin to see each test as a chance to grow! Just know that if He trusts you to overcome a battle, there's greater in store after your obedience. When the war is for God, the fight is never in vain.

Never underestimate the power of your testimony. God can always use your message to help someone else. Never in a million years did I think my ability to overcome promiscuity would be used to empower thousands via my blog! Now, people across the world email me about how much my story has changed their lives. When I first came to God, those initial moments of lust were the hardest to conquer. But, what was once just a moment of temptation is now a means by which God inspires people to become abstinent and live for Him. All across the world, those desiring to overcome my former struggles can be blessed by my experiences through Christ. So, never scorn God for bringing you to a battle. Your life is not about you, it's about those you're assigned to. Your victory can always be someone else's inspiration towards triumph.

For the many of us who want our lives to feel more fulfilled, we have to honestly examine ourselves. How do we respond to temptation? Part of having the true peace of God is fighting battles His way. If we would just ask God for help instead of trying to handle a situation on our own, we'd be surprised how quick He is to come in and save us. If we never involve God in any of the wars that we encounter, how can we have His peace when the battle is over?

Let's remember that to God all temptation and sin is the same. We need to be truthful with ourselves about what we need help with. Then, we must be bold enough to tell God how much we need Him. People often focus their attention on *what* a person is struggling with. But, in reality, *how* we handle our battles speaks louder than the battle itself. We must ask God to guide us in order to conquer the temptation that's in front of us. Then, we must trust His guidance.

Simply believing in God and hearing a Sunday sermon about His abilities to conquer our situations isn't enough. We have to apply God's Word to our lives on a daily basis. We must *live* what we read. *Each* time we run into an obstacle, we must realize that we *need* Him to overcome that moment. Let's not allow the devil, or anyone else, to tell us righteous living is impossible. Temptation is no match for us because of the God that lives in us. We can overcome today!

A Call from the Altar

If you are a sinner, please pray the following prayer and receive Jesus Christ into your life this very moment. He's waiting for you.

God, I come before you now in the name of Jesus Christ. I confess that I am a sinner and I want to be saved from my sins. I don't want to continue in this life of sin. Jesus Christ is Your Son and He died for my sins. God, You raised Him from the dead!

Jesus, I want You! I really need you right now and forever! I invite You into my heart right now. I accept You into my heart right now. Come in and live in me now!

I believe that You have come into my heart and life!

God, all these things I have asked and prayed in the name of Jesus Christ! Thank you for these and all other blessings! I will live for You and You alone! In Jesus Christ's name I pray, amen!

I AM SAVED!

About the Author

In 2014, Jordone created the *Jordonewrites* blog with a purpose to help women deepen their relationships with God. Having grown up around religious traditions, Jordone had always known about God, but she didn't know God. In 2012, God led Jordone on a personal journey where she began to discover God for herself. Gradually, she began to understand that there was more to God than just believing in Him and that God wanted an actual relationship with His children that continued beyond Sunday morning.

Her experiences led her to write her first book, *I Believe in God, Now What?*, a candid depiction of the challenges that Jordone experienced prior to her life with the Lord. Often called bold for its discussion of taboo topics, *Jordonewrites* is just a glimpse of the way God uses Jordone's writing as a light for others. Humbled to have been delivered from drugs, alcohol abuse, fornication, and the guilt of rape, Jordone's writing aims to let others know they aren't alone, hoping they'll understand they can come to God just as they are.

Jordonewrites has received attention from across the world, including well-known radio personality Michael Baisden. A native of Orangeburg, SC and alumna of Spelman College, Jordone currently works as a public speaker. She's also the co-editor of *Understanding: All Success is Attained by It*, by Dr. Shane Wall. As an editor and award-winning writer, she enjoys using her gift to help others tell their stories. Having lived in Africa and Spain, she enjoys traveling and learning about other cultures. In her spare time, she enjoys speaking with the youth and women in her community.

Contact

Jordone Branch

www.jordonewrites.com

- facebook.com/Jordonewrites
- twitter.com/jordonewrites
- linkedin.com/in/jordonebranch
- Periscope: jordonewrites
- instagram.com/jordonewrites

www.ingramcontent.com/pod-product-compliance
Lightning Source LLC
Chambersburg PA
CBHW052030290426
44112CB00014B/2447